M000024158

THEN & NOW

REDWOOD CITY

OPPOSITE: Rix and McLachlan's Garage was located at 302 Arguello Street, between Marshall and Bradford Streets. The garage was built in 1907 as the motorcar was becoming increasingly popular. Of interest is the shop's location directly across from the railroad tracks. (Photograph courtesy Redwood City Public Library.)

THEN & NOW

REDWOOD CITY

Nicholas A. Veronico, Betty S. Veronico,
Reg McGovern, and Janet McGovern

This book is dedicated to Mary K. "Molly" Spore-Alhadef as well as the staff and volunteers of the Redwood City Public Library and the San Mateo County Historical Association who work daily to preserve our history.

Copyright © 2010 by Nicholas A. Veronico, Betty S. Veronico, Reg McGovern, and Janet McGovern
ISBN 978-0-7385-8038-8

Library of Congress Control Number: 2009939078

Published by Arcadia Publishing
Charleston SC, Chicago IL, Portsmouth NH, San Francisco CA

Printed in the United States of America

For all general information contact Arcadia Publishing at:
Telephone 843-853-2070
Fax 843-853-0044
E-mail sales@arcadiapublishing.com
For customer service and orders:
Toll-Free 1-888-313-2665

Visit us on the Internet at www.arcadiapublishing.com

ON THE FRONT COVER: These photographs are of the San Mateo County Courthouse, then and now. Downtown revitalization saw the demolition of the 1939 Works Project Administration's Fiscal Building, which sat in front of the courthouse. The Fiscal Building's removal in 2005 opened up Courthouse Square, enabling the area to host large civic events, including a summer concert series as well as a variety of street fairs. Contrast the restored courthouse of today with the vintage photograph that shows the building within weeks of its June 23, 1910, opening. (Now photograph by Reg McGovern; then photograph courtesy Bradshaw Collection.)

ON THE BACK COVER: This intersection of Main Street and Broadway Street is seen in 1887, looking northeast toward the bay. Note the sails of multiple sloops seen at the end of Main Street. The building at left with the covered sidewalks is the Grand Hotel. (Photograph courtesy Redwood City Public Library.)

CONTENTS

ACKNOWLEDGMENTS

The authors wish to thank the following for their assistance in preparing this book: Cecilia Alipate; Robert Anderson; Rachel and David Anderson; Dominique, Sheridan, Dante, and Cheyenne Anderson; Dave Belasco; Joe and Virginia Biddle; Genny Biggs; Caroline and Ray Bingham; Cheryl Bracco; Claire and Joe Bradshaw; Arlene and Rich Bradshaw; Michelle Conci; Rhonda and Bruce Cumming; Raymond Dawley; Pat Dixon; John Edmonds; Richard Fuentes; Mike Giari; Patricia McRae; Jo Anne Montoya; Gordon Moore; Kathleen M. O'Connor; Bill O'Hanlon; Ethan Petersen; Mitch Postel; John Poultney; Carol Peterson; Carolyn Rapier; Shirley Schworer; Hank Sciaroni; Marsha Sims; Malcolm Smith; Don Snaman; Tabitha Snyder; Ana Solorio; Mary K. Spore-Alhadef; and Karen and Armand Veronico.

INTRODUCTION

Then & Now: *Redwood City* follows on the heels of the authors' highly successful Images of America: *Redwood City* (Arcadia Publishing, 2008). The changes that have taken place throughout the decades on the streets and avenues of the county seat needed photographic documentation to tell its story properly. Redwood City started as a sleepy logging town, grew to the San Mateo County seat, and entering the 21st century, has morphed into a much-desired suburb for a diverse population.

In its early days, Redwood City was part of the Rancho de las Pulgas, a 35,420-acre rancho owned by Don Dario Arguello. In 1854, Arguello's widow, Dona Maria Soledad Ortega Arguello, began selling off parts of the property. Simon Montserrate Mezes, the Arguello's attorney, was given one-fourth of the rancho for his service to the family. The Arguellos and Mezes donated much of the area that would become Redwood City's downtown to the people of California. A direct result of this gift was that in 1856 Redwood City was chosen as the San Mateo County seat. The first of four county courthouses was built on one of the parcels donated by Mezes, known at the time as California Square. Having been named the county seat, influential people began moving to the Redwood City area to fill government jobs.

As the area's logging business boomed and the San Francisco-to-San Jose train tracks were completed, the sleepy little town of Redwood City grew by leaps and bounds. By 1868, Redwood City had incorporated in order to maintain the city's infrastructure. The climate lured people to make their residence in town, and many San Francisco socialites began purchasing land and building summer homes to get away from the foggy days of the big city.

By the 1950s, the area along Woodside Road was developed, and Redwood City had transformed into a major suburban city. In the early 1980s, the city had expanded into Redwood Shores, adding more than 1,000 homes and a thriving commercial area to the city's boundaries.

Today Redwood City is home to many high-tech industries. The downtown is undergoing a tremendous transformation from a shuttered retail district to a thriving destination with boutiques and unique restaurants and cafés.

What was *then* a dusty port terminal for the logging industry is *now* one of the best places to live, work, and shop on the San Francisco Peninsula.

BUSINESS CENTER OF THE PENINSULA

This photograph of downtown looking toward Sequoia High School is seen from the top of the Fiscal Building at the north corner of Broadway and Hamilton Streets c. 1948. Across Hamilton Street is Burts women's wear, and on the south side of Broadway Street is Montgomery Ward. Notice the "W" cast into the facade of the Ward's building above the five second-story windows. On the same side of the street, across Winslow Street, is Woolworth's five-and-dime store. In the distance, the Redwood City Tribune Newspapers building (with flag flying) and, to its left, the Redwood Theater can be seen on the corner of California and Winklebeck Streets. (Photograph by Reg McGovern.)

At one time, Redwood Creek was navigable past Broadway Street. Opened in July 1859 by John Voger Diller, the Old Pioneer Store at 726 Main Street had facades that were the same on both sides of the building. If one approached from the street, one saw the same building as if one had sailed up Redwood Creek. In 1887, Philander P. Chamberlain (second from left) acquired the store, and he is seen with H. W. Schaberg, third from left, who was county clerk from 1903 to 1907, and George Holden, fourth from left. (Then photograph courtesy Redwood City Public Library; now photograph by Nicholas A. Veronico.)

Opened in 1872 as the Wentworth Tannery, the business was acquired by S. H. Frank two years later. The business was still in full operation when this 1958 view of Frank's Tannery was taken. Note the young man fishing from the banks of Redwood Creek. Today this area is the back side of the Kohl's Plaza near Veterans Boulevard and Walnut Street. (Then photograph courtesy Redwood City Public Library; now photograph by Nicholas A. Veronico.)

Henry Beeger acquired the tannery located at El Camino Real and Maple Street in 1880. The business was family owned and operated until 1947, and two years later the tannery was razed to reuse the property. Today the Towne Motor Company storage yard occupies the former Beeger Tannery property. (Then and now photographs by Reg McGovern.)

Cullen Feed and Fuel at 348 Main Street is pictured in 1925 with Fire Station No. 1 to the left and an adjoining storefront that at one time was home to a Spreckels Ice Cream shop, The Burwell Twins, and a cigar store. Today the 1.76-acre property is the City Center Plaza, completed in 1997, which houses a 74-unit, transit-oriented, mixed-use development with retail and restaurants on the ground floor and living spaces above. (Then photograph courtesy Redwood City Public Library; now photograph by Nicholas A. Veronico.)

Not much has changed with the Holmquist Hardware annex on Stambaugh Street. The business was started in 1895 by Rudolph Holmquist and was originally known as R. C. Holmquist Tinning and Plumbing. This building at 114 Stambaugh Street served as a machine shop for the thriving hardware business for more than 60 years. (Then photograph courtesy Redwood City Public Library; now photograph by Nicholas A. Veronico.)

Hull Brothers Hardware was located at what is now the corner of Broadway Street and Main Street, at 209 Main Street, across from the Sequoia Hotel. At the time, Broadway Street did not extend past Main Street. Today a new building housing the University of California at Berkeley Extension campus occupies the site. (Then photograph courtesy Redwood City Public Library; now photograph by Nicholas A. Veronico.)

These pictures (and those on the facing page) visually capture the progression of the city's first incorporated bank, which later merged with Wells Fargo Bank. Established in 1891, the domed First National Bank of San Mateo was located at the corner of Broadway Street and Main Street. Notice the Capitol Hotel two doors to the west. Today the bank building serves as offices for a number of professional service providers ranging from attorneys to certified public accountants. (Then photograph courtesy Redwood City Public Library; now photograph by Nicholas A. Veronico.)

A new First National Bank of San Mateo office opened across from the original domed building location on Main Street in 1941 (seen here as the middle building). The rectangular building fronted Broadway Street, and a parking lot was located on the east side of the new bank. First National Bank of San Mateo was acquired by Wells Fargo in the early 1970s, and in 1975, a new Wells Fargo branch was constructed in the old bank's parking lot. Once the new Wells Fargo branch was opened, the First National building was demolished and turned into a parking lot. (Then and now photographs by Reg McGovern.)

Christmas decorations liven up an overcast day along Broadway Street during the 1948 holiday season. Bunting and wreaths stretch from the Fiscal Building to the Sequoia Theater while holiday shoppers move about the streets. This, the second Sequoia Theater on Broadway Street, opened in 1929 and could seat 1,400 patrons. In 1950, the theater's name was changed to the Fox. Today the Fiscal Building is gone and the area has been given a new lease on life as Courthouse Square. (Then and now photographs by Reg McGovern.)

The building at 2022 and 2024 Broadway Street was originally home to the San Mateo County Building and Loan Association, as seen here around 1948. Note that the company's name has been cast into the facade above the first floor center windows. Today the sidewalks have been widened and trees planted to put some shade on the street. (Then and now photographs by Reg McGovern.)

The place to take a car for service or interior work was Kings Upholstery on El Camino Real and Diller Street. Notice how many businesses along El Camino Real had gas pumps and how the look of El Camino Real has changed with the addition of medians in the center of the street. Today the building has been modified but still retains its lines from the 1950s. (Then and now photographs by Reg McGovern.)

Jordan Paint Store Inc., founded in 1947 by brothers Walter and Don, was located on James Avenue. Two years later, the business, thriving in the post–World War II economy, moved to 837 Jefferson Avenue in the Redwood Plaza Shopping Center area of downtown. Notice the large Pacific Gas and Electric Company's 100-foot-by-100-foot natural gas tank, which dominated the city's skyline until 1960. Today Tarboosh, a restaurant serving Lebanese cuisine, operates in the same location. Redwood City's climate makes Tarboosh one of many great places for alfresco dining. (Then photograph by Reg McGovern; now photograph by Nicholas A. Veronico.)

In 1954, Reinhard and Company Jewelers was the anchor store on the north corner of Middlefield Road and Broadway Street facing the J. C. Penny's location that filled the opposite side of the street. Pacific Gas and Electric Company (PG&E) was two doors to the east. Today the corner is home to the ever-popular Bob's Courthouse Coffee Shop in the same location at 2198 Broadway Street. (Then and now photographs by Reg McGovern.)

Formerly an appliance store and gas station, Anderson's Service and Appliance outgrew this location on the corner of Jefferson Avenue and 1200 El Camino Real. The company moved three blocks down to 901 El Camino Real at the site of the former Redwood Theater. Today 1200 El Camino Real is home to a movie rental company and a coffee roasting company. Note that the barn-style roof of the residence at 1217 Jefferson Avenue has not changed and has only been overshadowed by the apartment building to the west. (Then photograph by Reg McGovern; now photograph by Nicholas A. Veronico)

For decades, Redwood City was known far and wide for its floral industry and nurseries, which were centered along both sides of Woodside Road and along Redwood Avenue, Valota Road, and the Horgan Ranch property. Many of the growers and greenhouse owners were Japanese Americans, and Redwood City's chrysanthemum growers were among the most successful in the country. Greenhouses produced a multimillion-dollar floral bonanza and were a point of pride for city residents. Pressed by competition, the high cost of energy, and escalating land values, the greenhouses eventually were replaced by residential development. (Then and now photographs by Reg McGovern.)

Redwood City was embarked on a postwar building boom in 1946 when Brooks Furniture opened at the corner of Stafford Street and what was then known as Rogers Street (now Whipple Avenue). Minus a tower, today's Any Mountain ski and sporting goods store is still recognizable as the same building. The store has been at this location for many years. (Then and now photographs by Reg McGovern.)

The Franklin Street residential community opened in 2002 and was heralded as a shining example of a public-private partnership. But today's residents might be surprised to know that a building materials firm called Redwood Material Company once covered the majority of the site. Cement trucks are lined up in the foreground of this 1949 picture, and a rail spur also served the site where cement, aggregate, and other products were brought in. (Then and now photographs by Reg McGovern.)

In the 1940s, industrial businesses like Progress Lumber Company were a common sight on El Camino Real. Progress Lumber, which sold both heavy construction building materials as well as consumer products, closed in 1965 and was razed along with several other businesses to make way for a Gemco discount store. Charter Street was widened and a left-turn lane was installed in 1966 to accommodate the traffic. A Target store is on the former Gemco site today. (Then and now photographs by Reg McGovern.)

Construction began for the Bekins Van and Storage Company building in 1951 at 1441 El Camino Real and finished in March of the following year. When the business opened, the 38,000-square-foot, five-story structure was the tallest habitable building in the city (only the PG&E gas tower was taller). Today the mezzanine of the building is home to Chain Reaction Bicycles, while Security Public Storage now provides storage services. (Then and now photographs by Reg McGovern.)

CHAPTER 2

COUNTY SEAT

Looking east toward the Dumbarton Bridge from the top of the San Mateo County Courthouse in 1946, the county jail can be seen across Middlefield Road. The giant 500,000-cubic-foot low-pressure gas tower owned and operated by Pacific Gas and Electric stands tall along Jefferson Avenue. Notice how Redwood Creek flows behind the tank, under the Bradford Street drawbridge to the left, and out toward the bay. The jail was removed and replaced with the new Brendan P. Maguire Correctional Facility at 300 Bradford Avenue in the mid-1980s. (Photograph by Reg McGovern.)

The present site of the San Mateo County Hall of Justice had been a park called California Square before the city deeded it over to accommodate county government growth. The move assured that county government would remain in the city where it had been located since 1856, rather than another site. This 1953 view is at the corner of Marshall and Hamilton Streets, looking north, and Allerton Street is at the top of the picture. (Then and now photographs by Reg McGovern.)

Beginning in the early 1920s, a tuberculosis sanitarium located in a canyon near Edgewood Road and Crestview Drive cared for patients living in bungalows. The Canyon Tuberculosis Sanitarium was demolished in 1950 and replaced in the same area with a $1.6 million, 116-bed San Mateo County Sanitarium, which became a psychiatric facility in the mid-1970s. The Cordilleras Mental Health Rehabilitation Center today is a 120-bed facility that contracts with the county to provide services. (Then and now photographs by Reg McGovern.)

A half-dozen cars and a motorcycle are lined up for a beauty shot outside the California Highway Patrol (CHP) office in 1937, then located on Marshall Street at Middlefield Road, across the street from the county fire department. A vacant office building occupies that site today. The companion photograph shows CHP cruisers and motorbikes today, ready to roll outside the headquarters at 355 Convention Way. (Then and now photographs by Reg McGovern.)

COUNTY SEAT

Located at the corner of Middlefield Road and Jefferson Avenue, today's city hall complex replaced the city's second city hall and the former library, which were built in 1939. The library relocated across the street to a new two-story building in 1992, and city staff moved into the old library space. Both city hall and the old library were torn down and a beautiful new city hall opened in 1997. (Then and now photographs by Reg McGovern.)

The arches for three fire engine bays are architectural elements that were retained when the 1920 main firehouse was renovated as a new main library. The 1947 view shows the firehouse when new white fire trucks arrived, replacing venerable red ones after 30 years. Poole Transfer and Storage, a moving company, was on the site where the children's wing of the library is today. The chamber of commerce building was later built on the corner. (Then and now photographs by Reg McGovern.)

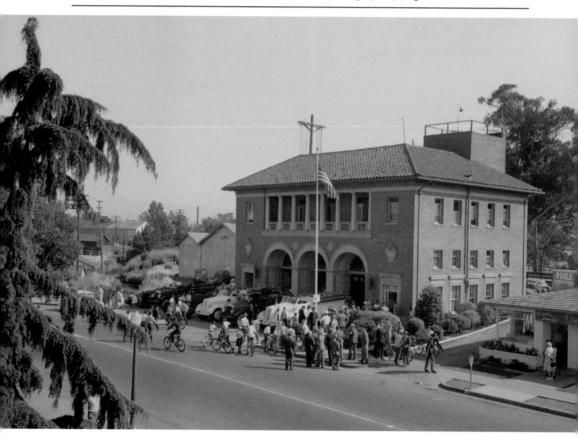

COUNTY SEAT

Shown here in 1955, Fire Station No. 2, on the corner of Jefferson Avenue and Myrtle Street, was constructed in 1928 with room for two trucks. The Spanish-style fire house was razed in 1981, and its larger, three truck bay replacement structure was completed the following year. The station's designation was also changed from No. 2 to No. 10 at the same time. (Then photograph by Reg McGovern; now photograph by Nicholas A. Veronico.)

When this San Mateo County Forest Service truck was photographed in 1937, vital public safety services were in the heart of downtown. Today San Mateo County Fire/CAL FIRE personnel and their equipment are based at a station on Edmonds Road, near their main response areas in the western hills of Redwood City and San Carlos and Interstate 280. The downtown Bank of America and its parking lot occupy the old fire department site. (Then and now photographs by Reg McGovern.)

Built in 1957 to house 42 employees, the 12,000-square-foot police department was located across from city hall on Middlefield Road. The department had grown to 117 full-time employees by 1993 when a new 40,000-square-foot headquarters opened. It lies east of the Bayshore Freeway on Maple Street on the site of a model airplane park and next to the former wastewater treatment plant. Library and city parking is now on the old police department location. (Then and now photographs by Reg McGovern.)

Gordon Moore, cofounder of Intel Corporation, grew up in Redwood City and was a 1946 graduate of Sequoia High School. His father, San Mateo County undersheriff Walter Moore, amassed a collection of more than 300 badges—including the tiny one in this 1948 photograph—during his 40-year career in law enforcement. After Walter's death, the Moore family donated the collection to the San Mateo County History Museum, where the badges are on display in Courtroom A. (Then and now photographs by Reg McGovern.)

The post office at 855 Jefferson Avenue was constructed in a Spanish-style motif in 1935, the same year this photograph was taken. Little has changed with the front of the building except for the addition of an awning over the entry doors and a wheelchair accessible ramp. Redwood Creek runs under the parking lot directly behind the post office and flows out under the driveway by the Suisha House under Broadway Avenue. (Then photograph courtesy Redwood City Public Library; now photograph by Nicholas A. Veronico.)

Huge concrete pipes were installed in the early 1950s as part of a multimillion-dollar expansion of the Hetch Hetchy water system by the City of San Francisco. The pipeline extended from San Francisco Bay to Moffett Field and eventually through the Emerald Lake area of Redwood City to Spring Valley Lake off Canada Road. This covered section is located off Jefferson Avenue in the vicinity of the Peninsula Covenant Church community center. (Then and now photographs by Reg McGovern.)

Built in 1931 at 2120 Broadway Street, the Pacific Gas and Electric Company's Redwood City office served the community for years. The building to the right is the original Sequoia Theater, and to the left today is Bob's Courthouse Coffee Shop. (Then photograph courtesy Redwood City Public Library; now photograph by Reg McGovern.)

Although only occupied by the phone company for less than five years, this building at 830 Middlefield Road served as the city's voice connection to the outside world. Pacific Telephone and Telegraph moved from this location to El Camino Real and Winslow Street in 1955. The downtown revitalization has brought a number of new businesses to the Theater District. Today the old phone company building is home to the highly rated Café La Tartine. (Then photograph by Reg McGovern; now photograph by Nicholas A. Veronico.)

GETTING AROUND TOWN

When the San Francisco-to-San Jose railroad was completed, a depot was needed in Redwood City. This original depot, built in 1901, was located on the east side of the tracks between Broadway and Winslow Streets; note the Redwood City Public School and its clock tower in the background. The depot was remodeled in 1937 and moved west, across the tracks. (Photograph courtesy Redwood City Public Library.)

Passenger trains have served Redwood City since 1863, operated for more than a century by the Southern Pacific Railroad. A three-county agency is responsible for the rail service known today as Caltrain. And although passengers' business attire may have changed radically over the generations, multitasking is not new: note the man on the right in 1951 seems to be looking at his watch, while his 2009 counterpart appears to be text-messaging. (Then and now photographs by Reg McGovern.)

GETTING AROUND TOWN

This 1950 scene shows crews repairing track at the Broadway Street railroad crossing. On the right is the Quonset hut–shaped Purity grocery store. A flagman in a tiny hut next to the tracks would come out to wave a red flag when trains approached. On the left is the Southern Pacific freight shed. Around 2000, Caltrain upgraded the Redwood City station, installing platforms lined with brick pavers, a center fence, and smoother-riding concrete railroad ties. (Then and now photographs by Reg McGovern.)

GETTING AROUND TOWN

Some things never seem to change—including crowds and lines at the local California Department of Motor Vehicles office. In 1953, early birds who tried to escape lines at the Redwood City DMV at Whipple Avenue and Arguello Street to obtain new license "tabs" found that others had the same idea. Today's DMV office, located at 300 Brewster Avenue, keeps just as busy in today's auto-dependent culture. Royal Cleaners is in the old DMV building. (Then and now photographs by Reg McGovern.)

GETTING AROUND TOWN

When parking meters debuted in 1947, motorists initially got "courtesy notices" while they became familiar with the need to feed pennies and nickels into the new color-coded meters. By the time this picture was taken in 1953, parking meters were old hat. In 2007, high-tech parking meters that could even be "fed" from cell phones introduced the learning curve anew. Businessmen Larry Rhodes is shown here putting money into the solar-powered meter. (Then and now photographs by Reg McGovern.)

Earl Whitmore (who later became San Mateo County sheriff) pointed to termite-ridden boards that in 1947 necessitated the closure of a bridge over Bradford Street, which connected Jefferson Avenue and Main Street. The bridge did not open again until seven years later after a $10,000 rebuilding project. In the 1960s, the creek was channeled into a culvert and was paved over. At the top of the modern photograph, Kaiser Hospital and its parking garage are visible, and the Redwood City School District office is on the right. (Then and now photographs by Reg McGovern.)

GETTING AROUND TOWN

Ely Chrysler Plymouth was located on the corner of Claremont Avenue and El Camino Real, northeast of Whipple Avenue. Owner Leonard Ely used to showcase his new models on the triangular median in front of the dealership until the city landscaped the pie-shaped piece of property. Today the Standard Station has been replaced by a 7-11 food store, and the Redwood City sign is a lot smaller and has been moved to the median. (Then photograph by Reg McGovern; now photograph by Nicholas A. Veronico.)

Before a modern Bayshore Freeway was extended down the peninsula, turns onto the Bayshore Highway were risky, as this 1951 photograph shows. With no traffic signal at Whipple Avenue and "Old Bayshore," drivers had to navigate lanes of traffic to turn. The freeway was completed through Redwood City in mid-1958. "Old Bayshore" is now Veterans Boulevard, and traffic signals and turn lanes regulate the flow of traffic. (Then and now photographs by Reg McGovern.)

This is how the intersection of Fifth Avenue and the Southern Pacific railroad tracks appeared in 1949, when two automobiles barely had enough room to pass on the 20-foot-wide street. Fifth Avenue became the first Redwood City railroad crossing to be grade-separated after voters in 1988 approved a half-cent sales tax for transportation improvements. Both rail and pedestrian bridges were constructed as part of the $18 million project, completed in 1996. (Then photograph by Reg McGovern; now photograph by Nicholas A. Veronico)

Harry Bourquin, who had started out as a plasterer, built his own Bourquin Motors showroom and garage at 923 Jefferson Avenue, pictured here in 1947. The Hudson was billed as "the car you step *down* into" because it was just 5 feet from the ground to the top. Long after the dealership was history, the site made way for the Jefferson Avenue railroad grade separation project and is now a municipal parking lot. (Then and now photographs by Reg McGovern.)

Three thousand gardenias, plus cigars and hand lotion, were given away in 1953 to celebrate the remodeling of R&R Service, advertised as "Redwood City's most modern service station." Gene Bourquin operated the Mobil station at the corner of Middlefield Road and Main Street for nearly 40 years, until 1984. The station was later torn down when the City Center Plaza redevelopment project was built opposite the main library parking lot in the late 1990s. (Then and now photographs by Reg McGovern.)

Begun as a roadside filling station and auto repair shop, Nelson "Ed" Davies opened Davies Auto Company in 1916 on El Camino Real and Vera Avenue. The business relocated to Jefferson Avenue and El Camino Real in 1942 and is seen here in 1948. Brothers Al and Tom Davies renamed the business EZ Davies Chevrolet in 1954 and operated it until 1990, when the family sold the business. Davies Chevrolet and the surrounding businesses were bulldozed to make way for Sequoia Station, which opened in 1992. (Then photograph by Reg McGovern; now photograph by Nicholas A. Veronico.)

GETTING AROUND TOWN

In a scene reminiscent of today, bus riders in 1964 boarded Peninsula Transit Lines Routes A and B, in proximity to the train station platform. Municipal and private bus lines throughout the county were replaced after the San Mateo County Transit District was established in 1976 to provide county-wide bus service. Today SamTrans and Caltrain offer a convenient intermodal connection at the train station. (Then and now photographs by Reg McGovern.)

SamTrans' Brewster Avenue bus facility today is home base for part of the transit district's fleet operating between San Francisco and Palo Alto, as well as the administrative center for Redi-Wheels paratransit service. In an earlier era, residents relied on buses from Pacific Greyhound Lines to commute to San Francisco and points beyond. The Greyhound depot was located in the same place where it is today. SamTrans took over the former Greyhound commuter service between San Francisco and Palo Alto in 1977. (Then and now photographs by Reg McGovern.)

GETTING AROUND TOWN

The building that for 35 years has been the home of Roosevelt Liquor and Groceries has not changed much since this photograph was taken. Roosevelt Avenue was on a bus route, just as it is today. In 1966, Harry Kramer opened his first Harry's Hofbrau in this building but relocated in 1968 to the current site two blocks south on El Camino Real. Aaron Brothers Art and Framing is visible on the opposite corner today. (Then and now photographs by Reg McGovern.)

The opening of the $4.25 million Woodside Expressway project in 1965 resolved long-standing traffic problems in the Five Points area, where bumper-to-bumper tie-ups on El Camino Real were everyday occurrences. Barely visible at the far left side of the earlier photograph is the "Climate Best" sign that stood near the Shell station where Harry's Hofbrau is today. Broadway Cleaners, a landmark local business at 1681 Main Street, can be seen in both views. (Then and now photographs by Reg McGovern.)

Recognizing that its deepwater shipping channel presented unique opportunities, Redwood City voters in 1936 "launched" the port as a separate municipal enterprise. Managed by its own commission, Redwood City's port has traditionally focused on bulk commodities such as lumber, cement, produce, aggregate, and scrap metal.

These aerial views show the growth of the port from the early 1950s to today, with the Pacific Shores corporate campus as a new neighbor. (Then photograph by Reg McGovern; now photograph courtesy Marsha Sims, Aurora Concept Associates via Port of Redwood City.)

In 1937, Walter F. Murphy, who had previously worked in the Pacific Northwest, became the port's first executive director. Murphy cultivated new commodities, notably Santa Clara Valley produce as an export and lumber from the Northwest as an import. Port director since 1995, Michael J. Giari had worked at East Coast ports prior to coming to Redwood City. In 2009, the port completed a major boat launch ramp upgrade and is planning for a $15 million project to replace a 60-year-old wooden wharf. (Then and now photographs by Reg McGovern.)

CHAPTER 4

REDWOOD CITY LIVING

Bounded by the railroad tracks on the top and El Camino Real at the bottom, this 1947 aerial view shows the area that today encompasses the Sequoia Station shopping center. James Avenue bisects the picture, with commuter parking on the left side. The former Davies Chevrolet dealership is on the lower right, and the Old Mill Flower Shop and a Texaco station are at the foot of James Avenue. Anchored by a Safeway and a Longs Drug store, Sequoia Station opened in 1995 on a 10.5-acre redevelopment site. The connection with SamTrans and Caltrain was a key component of the vision for the project, which included a transit terminal and a 315-space underground parking garage. (Photograph by Reg McGovern.)

The mansion of lumber tycoon Charles Hanson served during the 1920s and early 1930s as the convent for the Sisters of Notre Dame de Namur, California Province, who came to Redwood City in 1885 to establish Our Lady of Mount Carmel School. Located on a block bounded by Arguello, Fuller, and Warren Streets at Brewster Avenue, the house was torn down in 1949 for a business development. Today a medical office building occupies the site. (Then photograph courtesy Redwood City Public Library; now photograph by Reg McGovern.)

"Alhambra" and vicinity apr. 18. 1906

The Alhambra Theater at 831–835 Main Street was severely damaged in the 1906 San Francisco earthquake. Businesses small and large suffered, although most rebuilt. The small H. C. Offermann grocery was also hard hit. Notice the "Zon-o-phone" sign above the grocery, which advertised one of the first disc records—a revolution when everyone else was listening to cylinder records. The Alhambra Theater's facade was updated in the mid-1990s and a bronze plaque was added near the theater's door to mark its location. (Then photograph courtesy Redwood City Public Library; now photograph by Nicholas A. Veronico.)

The Sequoia Hotel was built on the site of the Eureka Brewery in the years after the 1906 San Francisco earthquake. When it opened in 1912, the hotel was the picture of opulence—each guest room had its own bathroom with hot and cold running water. This was quite a luxury as, at the time, most hotels had shared restroom facilities, typically one per floor. The hotel is seen here one year after it opened. When Pres. Herbert Hoover came to Redwood City for the Fourth of July Parade, he made the Sequoia Hotel his headquarters. Today new, upscale retailers have established themselves in the hotel's retail spaces. (Then photograph courtesy Redwood City Public Library; now photograph by Nicholas A. Veronico.)

James Stafford and brother Dan operated a grocery store from 1872 to 1926. Stafford Brothers General Merchandise was located on Broadway Street between Hamilton and Winslow Streets, as seen in this 1910 photograph. Businesses in that block changed numerous times over the years, and Chase Bank now occupies the property. (Then photograph courtesy Redwood City Public Library; now photograph by Nicholas A. Veronico.)

In this photograph taken around 1920, two Abyssinian lions created by a Belgian sculptor named Gef still stood at the entrance to a 163-acre development, planned in the late 1880s by the Wellesley Land and Improvement Company. Mounted on basalt pedestals, the lions remain at the entrance to the Wellesley Park subdivision today. Like generations of children, area resident Dave Belasco played on the Wellesley Crescent Park lion statues when he was a boy. (Then photograph courtesy Redwood City Public Library; now photograph by Reg McGovern.)

In the 1930s, Musso Drugs occupied the corner of Broadway Avenue and El Camino Real. By the late 1940s, the business had changed hands to Baird's Pharmacy, and the building's numerous signs were removed for this more streamlined look. In the 1960s, the building's Spanish-style facade was removed, producing the minimalist look of today's operator, Savada-Adamich Opticians. (Then photograph by Reg McGovern; now photograph by Nicholas A. Veronico.)

Hotel de Redwood is one of the longest surviving businesses in Redwood City. During the 1880s, Mrs. A. A. Kennedy was the hotel's proprietor when it was a popular stop for ranchers and cattlemen traveling to and from the city's port. After the turn of the 20th century, entrepreneur Antonio Bertolucci acquired the Hotel de Redwood along with the Oak Villa Hotel in Menlo Park. The property was reconstructed in the 1960s, and today it is operated as the Pacific Euro Hotel-Redwood City. (Then photograph courtesy Redwood City Public Library; now photograph by Reg McGovern.)

Construction of the Kaiser Permanente Medical Center was well underway when this November 28, 1967, photograph was taken. Forty years later, the hospital has expanded a number of times and occupies a large swath of property along Veterans Boulevard. (Then and now photographs by Reg McGovern.)

Main Street in 1951 was a thriving commercial street even without a two-and-a-half-hour Fourth of July Parade to attract 50,000 people to the city. Small businesses, including furniture and auto parts stores, sign shops, and restaurants, were typical of the Main Street mix. Despite the redevelopment that has changed the face of much of downtown, Main Street has retained many of its historic facades and retains an eclectic commercial character. (Then and now photographs by Reg McGovern.)

Piggy Wiggly grocery came to Redwood City in 1954 as the anchor tenant of the 5-Points shopping center. Notice the star with the number five above the Piggly Wiggly tower sign. The Rexall Drug Store is adjacent to the grocery, and now 55 years later, most chain grocers have incorporated pharmacies into their floor plans. Today Piggly Wiggly is gone and 5-Points has been extensively remodeled with Bed, Bath, and Beyond as the anchor tenant. (Then photograph by Reg McGovern; now photograph by Nicholas A. Veronico.)

In March 1952, the Safeway at 2200 El Camino Real was billed as the grocery chain's largest and most modern store on the peninsula. The store had originally been slated to open on June 6, 1951, however, a fire of unknown origin interrupted preparations on 6:14 p.m. on May 25, 1951. The fire severely damaged the structure and all of its contents, but Safeway was committed to Redwood City and rebuilt the store. Today Safeway is located down the El Camino Real at Sequoia Station, and U-Haul occupies the previous property. (Then photograph by Reg McGovern; now photograph by Nicholas A. Veronico.)

Woodside Plaza was developed in 1953 along the Woodside Road corridor. Originally, Lucky Market was on the south side. Today Thrifty is in the same location, but Lucky's has moved to the north end. Pet Food Express now occupies the original Lucky Market location. (Then photograph by Reg McGovern; now photograph by Nicholas A. Veronico.)

Looking east toward El Camino Real, this was the view of Jefferson Avenue in 1949, when an overhaul and repaving of the street from El Camino Real to Grand Street was under way at a cost of $9,000. At that time, Jefferson Avenue only extended west to the Emerald Lake Hills area of the city. Since widened, Jefferson Avenue today is a major east-west arterial through the city to the western hills, connecting to Interstate 280. (Then and now photographs by Reg McGovern.)

For decades, consumers have done their grocery shopping at stores on El Camino Real at Jefferson Avenue, on the site of a former estate. A Lucky store opened in 1962 and was replaced by a larger one in 1992. Times and tastes change, and in November 2004, Whole Foods Market, based in Austin, Texas, opened the doors of this 39,000-square-foot store, bringing its distinctive combination of natural and organic food to a new generation of consumers. (Then photograph by Reg McGovern; now photograph by Nicholas A. Veronico.)

This is the view of the front of Sequoia Hospital before the grand opening ceremony October 15, 1950, featuring then governor Earl Warren and other dignitaries heralding the arrival of an institution that has served the community for nearly 60 years. Opened as a 106-bed facility, the hospital added another 102-bed wing in 1954. Sequoia Hospital currently is undergoing a major seismic retrofit and reconstruction project, due for completion in spring 2013. (Then and now photographs by Reg McGovern.)

Located at 1833 Broadway Street, All American Super Market was a local favorite. Grocery Outlet Bargain Market has occupied the location for several years. The philosophy of the Grocery Outlet chain is to give back to the community. The manager of the Redwood City store donates to Habitat for Humanity and the local Boys and Girls Club, as well as many other local nonprofit organizations. (Then photograph by Reg McGovern; now photograph by Nicholas A. Veronico.)

The Marine World amusement park opened in 1968 at Redwood Shores, featuring aquatic entertainment including whale, dolphin, and seal shows. For two decades, the park, which later added "Africa U.S.A." to its name, provided chances to learn about animals and memorable job opportunities for local kids. In 1986, Marine World/Africa U.S.A. relocated to Vallejo. Its former site was redeveloped with office towers and has been the headquarters for Oracle Corporation since 1989. (Then photograph courtesy Redwood City Public Library; now photograph by Reg McGovern.)

CHAPTER 5

EDUCATION
AND WORSHIP

Our Lady of Mount Carmel Church, located at 301 Grand Street, was founded in 1887. Originally the church was under the jurisdiction of San Mateo's St. Matthew's parish with the oversight of Fr. Denis Dempsey. The first pastor was Fr. Daniel O'Sullivan, who was born in County Kerry, Ireland. For generations, the church served predominately local Irish and Italian families. Today the church's membership is as diverse as the city's. (Photograph courtesy Redwood City Public Library.)

This beautiful building was the Redwood City Public School, also known as the Grammar School. Built in 1895 at a cost of $23,000, it sat directly across from the courthouse. Elementary students were housed in the first two floors, and high school students occupied the third floor. The magnificent structure was demolished in 1927. Later the same year, the Sequoia Theater, renamed Fox Theatre in 1950, was opened. Today the site houses the 1,400-seat Fox Theatre, the Little Fox nightclub, and retail and office space. (Then photograph courtesy Redwood City Public Library; now photograph by Reg McGovern.)

EDUCATION AND WORSHIP

On July 15, 1904, Sequoia High School opened its doors in this grand building on Broadway Avenue with a student body of 53 members. In 1924, the high school students were moved to their new school at the corner of El Camino Real and Brewster Avenue, and grammar school students occupied this building until 1948. Today the newly developed theater and retail shops are a vital part of the city's downtown area. (Then and now photographs by Reg McGovern.)

Located at El Camino Real and Brewster Avenue, Sequoia High School's original 1924 construction consisted of a two-story L-shaped building, an auditorium, a boy's gymnasium, and two swimming pools. The school has consistently grown to accommodate the student population. The main entrance to Sequoia High School still proudly shows off Argo Tower, named for Clarence Argo, principal from 1921 to 1948. (Then photograph courtesy Veronico Collection; now photograph by Reg McGovern.)

EDUCATION AND WORSHIP

When Sequoia High School opened in downtown in 1895, it was the first public high school on the peninsula and had an enrollment of 53 students. The first 17 graduates donned their formal best for this 1898 photograph, surely not seeing themselves as pioneers in a great academic tradition. One hundred and eleven years later, the class of 2009 graduated 256 students; attired in purple or white caps and gowns, they marched onto the football field for the traditional ceremony. (Then photograph courtesy Redwood City Library; now photograph by Reg McGovern.)

Lincoln School was one of the first schools built in Redwood City. Both Lincoln and Washington Schools were constructed in 1916 and were built thanks to a 1915 bond measure to provide for two new elementary schools. In 1974, the decision was made to close Lincoln School because of declining enrollment, and the school on Whipple Avenue and Oakdale Street was later razed and replaced by homes. (Then and now photographs by Reg McGovern.)

EDUCATION AND WORSHIP

Washington School was the second elementary school in Redwood City. Located at 485 Woodside Road, the school closed in 1979. The site now houses the Woodside Terrace Retirement Center, an independent and assisted living community for seniors. (Then photograph courtesy Redwood City Public Library; now photograph by Reg McGovern.)

John Gill Elementary School, located at 555 Avenue del Ora at Jefferson Avenue, currently serves 420 students in kindergarten through fifth grade. Built in 1932 in the French Provincial style, the school was named after Thomas Jefferson but was renamed in 1937 after school superintendent John Gill, who died suddenly that year. Note that today the high French-style roofs are gone and have been replaced by Spanish tiles. (Then photograph by Reg McGovern; now photograph by Nicholas A. Veronico.)

EDUCATION AND WORSHIP

The Garfield Charter School serves the North Fair Oaks district and is located at 3600 Middlefield Road. The school offers classes to preschool-age children through eighth grade, separated into two programs: kindergarten through fifth grade (elementary schools) and sixth through eighth grade (middle schools). (Then and now photographs by Reg McGovern.)

McKinley School opened its doors in January 1928 after the demolition of the landmark Central School downtown. Children living west of "the highway" (El Camino Real) between Redwood and Brewster Avenues went to McKinley. The clock in the old Central School tower was placed in the McKinley School tower, but in the 1950s, the tower came down as part of seismic upgrades. Now called McKinley Institute of Technology, the school serves students in grades six through eight. (Then photograph courtesy Redwood City Public Library; now photograph by Reg McGovern.)

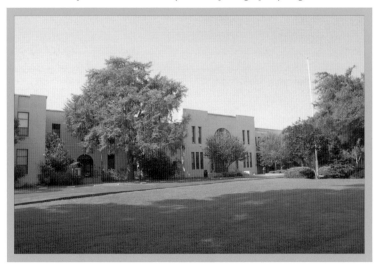

EDUCATION AND WORSHIP

For generations, Redwood City schools have offered students an excellent music program. This was the scene in 1948 as the McKinley School orchestra players rehearsed under the direction of Ronald Spink. The Redwood City School District maintains that tradition today with four instrumental music teachers and some 950 students. Pictured here in the spring of 2009, Tabitha Snyder directs the McKinley musicians. (Then and now photographs by Reg McGovern.)

Built in 1925, this church at Broadway Street and Brewster Avenue is the third location for the First United Methodist Church. The first was a 28-foot-by-42-foot structure built in 1865 in an area downtown known as "The Island" because of the confluence of two creeks. In 1873, a church on Maple Street replaced it. The present church was consecrated in 1951 upon the addition of a 500-seat sanctuary furnished with Philippine mahogany pews. (Then photograph courtesy Redwood City Public Library; now photograph by Reg McGovern.)

FIRST METHODIST CHURCH, REDWOOD CITY, CALIFORNIA   4341

EDUCATION AND WORSHIP

Built in 1960, the Sisters of St. Francis-Mt. Alverno Convent was constructed at 3910 Bret Harte Drive in the hills of Redwood City. It is a 100,000-square-foot, four-story building sitting on 25.7 acres. In 2003, the convent was sold to a Japanese Buddhist sect, Shinnyo-en. The Redwood City location is the head temple of Shinnyo-en in the United States. (Then photograph courtesy Redwood City Public Library; now photograph by Reg McGovern.)

Located off Woodside Road, Union Cemetery is a 6-plus-acre burial site for Civil War soldiers and local pioneers. For years, the abandoned cemetery suffered neglect, vandalism, and disrepair, evident in this 1947 photograph. Recognizing the unique historic asset for what it is, dedicated volunteers and the city united to restore the cemetery, which is listed on the National Register of Historic Places. In 1999, a bronze replica replaced the original Civil War Union soldier. (Then and now photographs by Reg McGovern.)

ABOUT THE AUTHORS

Preservation of local history through photography is a shared interest of the Veronicos and the McGoverns. Then and Now: *Redwood City* is the second collaboration by the four authors and is an extension of their research on their previous work Images of America: *Redwood City*. Both books are built around photographs of Redwood City and the surrounding areas gathered from numerous sources. One of the best sources are photographs taken by Reg McGovern beginning in 1937 and culminating with scenes of Redwood City today.

Coauthor Nicholas A. Veronico has written more than two dozen books on aviation, military, and local history subjects. This includes four previous titles for Arcadia Publishing—Images of Aviation: *Moffett Field,* 2006; Images of America: *World War II Shipyards by the Bay*, 2007; Images of America: *San Carlos*, 2007 (with Betty S. Veronico); and Images of America: *Redwood City*, 2008 (with Reg and Janet McGovern and Betty S. Veronico). He works on contract as a science writer at NASA Ames Research Center in Mountain View, California.

Coauthor Betty S. Veronico is a commercial property manager on the San Francisco Peninsula and is a Redwood City native. Her deep interest in lighthouses resulted in her first solo book Images of America: *Lighthouses of the Bay Area* (Arcadia Publishing, 2008), which examines lighthouse technology as well as 19 lighthouses and the lightships that have served the San Francisco Bay and its approaches. She previously collaborated on two additional books for Arcadia Publishing, Images of America: *San Carlos* (with Nicholas A. Veronico) and Images of America: *Redwood City* (with Reg and Janet McGovern and Nicholas A. Veronico.)

After a stint in the U.S. Coast Guard during World War II, Redwood City native Reg McGovern spent the rest of his career as an award-winning newspaper photographer for the *Redwood City Tribune*. Now retired, McGovern has opened up his catalog of photographs that begins in 1937 to help fill the pages of this volume and his previous work for Arcadia Publishing, Images of America: *Redwood City*. When not behind the camera, Reg enjoys listening to big band music.

Janet McGovern works as a marketing professional for the San Mateo County Transit District. Before joining that organization, she served as a reporter and columnist for the *Redwood City Tribune* and the *Peninsula Times Tribune*. Her work as a reporter gives her an interesting perspective on the events and personalities that helped shape Redwood City during the past 30 years.

www.arcadiapublishing.com

Discover books about the town where you grew up, the cities where your friends and families live, the town where your parents met, or even that retirement spot you've been dreaming about. Our Web site provides history lovers with exclusive deals, advanced notification about new titles, e-mail alerts of author events, and much more.

MADE IN THE USA

Arcadia Publishing, the leading local history publisher in the United States, is committed to making history accessible and meaningful through publishing books that celebrate and preserve the heritage of America's people and places. Consistent with our mission to preserve history on a local level, this book was printed in South Carolina on American-made paper and manufactured entirely in the United States.

This book carries the accredited Forest Stewardship Council (FSC) label and is printed on 100 percent FSC-certified paper. Products carrying the FSC label are independently certified to assure consumers that they come from forests that are managed to meet the social, economic, and ecological needs of present and future generations.

FSC
Mixed Sources
Product group from well-managed forests and other controlled sources

Cert no. SW-COC-001530
www.fsc.org
© 1996 Forest Stewardship Council

Find Your Place in History.